Dradnats and the SI Metric Measurement Kids

Dradnats and the SI Metric Measurement Kids

Linda S. Dawson

M any countries around the world have changed over to the International System of Units (SI), others have partially changed over, and still others are considering converting to SI. About 95% of countries use some form of SI. The many advantages of SI include: making conversions based on powers of ten, comparisons within the families (meter, Liter, gram) are easier, and the interchangeable names and prefixes of SI's meter, liter, and gram, make global communication and world trade easier. When it is mentioned that conversions are based on powers of ten, this makes the system easier than Standard Units of Measurement that we use in the United States.

Let's say in Standard we want to go from feet to inches. Let's take 3 ½ feet = _____ inches. First of all, you need to memorize all kinds of standard measurements that do not relate at all. You would need to know there are 12 inches in a foot. Twelve is not a power of ten, so you can't make a conversion by simply adding a zero, knocking off a zero, or moving a decimal point to the left or to the right. You have to *know* there are twelve inches in a foot. Then, you must multiply it by three, figure out how many inches in ½ foot, and add it together. Compare that conversion to metric -- 3 .5 cm = _____ mm Here, since mm is smaller than cm, one just multiplies by 10. Hence, 3.5 cm = 35 mm It is important to know one rule. As you increase by a power of ten, you simply add a zero: 1, 10,100, (1,000 which will be the basic meter, Liter, gram), 10,000, 100,000, 1,000,000. This "powers of ten" pattern is used over and over in simple conversions of the meter, Liter, and gram. At the back of this book will be exercises and step-by-step directions of how this works. Once you do a few, you will see how easy it is!

The International System of Units (SI) dominates the entire world as the preferred system of measurement. This book is designed to introduce all people who are unfamiliar with SI to the segment that deals with measurement (meter and gram) and also gives readers a small introduction to volume (liter) (3 dimensional). SI has many other facets; this book just serves as an introduction.

The United States uses Standard Units of Measurement (also called Customary) instead of SI. Although both systems are standardized, the measurement system that still uses feet, pounds, gallons, etc. will be referred to as Standard/Customary as opposed to SI. The ogre in this book, DRADNATS, is Standard (Customary) spelled backwards. It does not mean that Standard/Customary is a *bad* system of measurement; it's just a lot harder to learn and takes a lot more time to make conversions. There is no certainty that the U.S. will ever *go* metric, but our basic knowledge of it is not good, and we see metric measurements every single day. It would be beneficial to understand it a little bit, right? It is the author's hope that you will derive some basic information with just a couple readings of the little story and some serious practice on the problems at the back.   Let's learn this measurement system – SI!

In the land of Metrica lies the fate of 18 fascinating children. The **Liters', Grams',** and **Meters'** families are marooned on a lifeless, arid side of a once roaring river. They had intended to be gone just one week. They had made week long excursions many times before, so they knew to bring along plenty of food, drinking water, and use the survival skills they had been taught.

What the parents and children didn't realize was that the City of Metrica was planning on **draining** the river to build a more modern water facility and a giant dam. The newspaper's plan was to publish the news that very day the kids embarked on their venture!

They were excited to reach this unknown territory. Even so, soon after setting up camp, they watched, before their very eyes, the surging river recede as the sun pounded down on the river's bottom. It took just a few hours for the river's bottom to become parched, cracked, and full of sink holes. Their raft was hopelessly stuck!

When they realize their predicament, they are stunned. They desperately want to get back to the other side where their parents would be worried and waiting for them. The kids have no idea they have reached an area where a feared, giant ogre lives.

The monster's name is Dradnats! His face is ugly with incredible eyes. The eyes can bulge out and get so large that he can count all the craters on the moon! In the next second, they can become slits so small, they look like tiny black horizontal lines on his hideous face and make him able to see things tinier than a period on a page!

The children *should* fear him! He can push out his eyeballs, peek through dense bushes, and see the nine brothers who are hundreds of times bigger than their sisters. In a blink of an eye, Dradnats can squint really hard, look down an insect hole, and closely watch the very tiny nine sisters.

Dradnats has a plan to capture them all and take them back to his cave. He will start a gigantic fire pit and throw all of them in to flavor his daily soup. Dradnats wonders, "How did they find *his* territory?" He heard of these families and wants nothing to do with them! He knew that these three families live in the city of Metrica.

Each of the families has the same names for the sisters and brothers. The three sweet little daughters are: **Milli, Centi,** and **Deci.** The kind and gentle (but quite large) sons in each family are: **Deka, Hecto,** and **Kilo.**

One day, while hiding from the ogre, **Milli Liter,** the tiniest of the **Liter** family, finds a little bitty drop of water on a leaf. What a surprise in such a dry land! She mixes it with a **milligram** of sand, and **Milli Liter and Milli Gram** drop the mixture at the raft's edge. They hope it pushes the raft forward to home, but, unfortunately, the raft slides ahead just a **millimeter**. That is such a *tiny* distance! Since it is *very roughly* the width of an eyelash, it doesn't look like the boat has moved at all!

That afternoon, **Centi Liter** finds a small puddle at the entrance of a cave. She mixes a **centiliter** of water with a **centigram** of sand and eagerly pushes it under the raft. The raft just moves a **centimeter**. An easy way to remember a **centimeter** is to think of it as *about* the width of a small finger! That's hardly any movement!

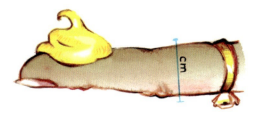

The following night as the family looks for shelter from the ogre, **Deci Liter** comes upon a swamp full of murky water. The eighteen kids have no idea that the ogre is hiding in the tall thorny bushes watching everything they do. Yet, they sense something is not right. **Deci** mixes a **deciliter** of water with a **decigram** of sand and plops the goop at the boat. Ah! The raft advances a **decimeter**. Think of a **decimeter** as being *approximately* the length of a brand new crayon. **Deci** sighs. That distance is not *nearly* enough distance to get back to their homeland!

dm

Their predicament becomes worse. The city of Metrica has now drained the water from the river. Many areas are dry, but there are also many enormous sinkholes that are hidden by thin layers of dried mud. Some of the brothers and sisters try to cross the river's bottom and are almost sucked in! They watch a large bird enjoying a walk across the terrain only to make a wrong step and be swallowed whole! There is no *way* they are going to get back to Metrica by walking!

They encounter another problem. There are giant footprints with claws that could only have been left by the feared ogre. People in Metrica had talked about a monster in this general area. A few had seen him and were repulsed by his creepy eyes. They didn't know that, with his extraordinary vision, Dradnats could see every single one of them – even over in the land of **SI**. (Remember **SI** is the International System of Units used by at least 95% of people in the world.)

The ogre's left eye can bulge out and see great distances. He has no problem seeing the **Kilo** brothers. The ogre's tiny right eye can squint and see teeny distances – like the size of **Milli**, **Centi**, and **Deci**. The **Kilo** brothers are a *million* times bigger than their **Milli** sisters, so this ogre has really sophisticated eyes!

The children are distraught! They can't get home, and they're in the land ruled by Dradnats! Their shelters become very secretive and camouflaged to hide from him. They must stay on the move to confuse him. The swamp offers thick branches to prepare for their next hideout.

Deka Liter and **Deka Gram** wander off to find more water and sand to propel the boat. In their search, they come upon a pool of bubbling stinky water. Little do they know that this is where the ogre bathes. As the others sleep, they mix a **dekaliter** of nasty water and a **dekagram** of dirty sand and bring it over to the raft. It juts forward a whole **dekameter**. Have you ever seen a giant city bus? One could say the bus is *very roughly* a **dekameter** long. Sadly, that distance is *still* not enough to return to their parents!

The two **Dekas** sadly look out toward their homeland. The Metric SI Kids have tried to push the raft a millimeter, a centimeter, a decimeter, a meter, and a dekameter. Nothing is working. It's just not enough water and sand to send the boat forward! They realize that the boat will have to thrust ahead **so** hard that it will slide quickly to Metrica that is still quite a distance away.

As they migrate to yet another hiding place, they come upon a large rocky ridge. There are deep cracks. These crevices give just enough room to squeeze in and be warm and safe. As the kids get comfy in their hiding place, **Hecto Liter** and **Hecto Gram** become restless. The boys want to continue to try to solve their problem. Where in the world can they find enough water and sand to pour under the boat and boost it forward?

They have an idea. They climb up the large ridge just above their heads. Rocks of all sizes dislodge and tumble down. The boys are giving up hope of finding water. Finally, they reach the summit and see a gigantic puddle of water and a larger body of water further in the distance. They also see quite a bit of sand.

The huge puddle is enough water to *possibly* fill a large bathtub. Is *this* puddle enough water and sand to propel the raft? The sand around the puddle looks to be a few ounces. The two **Hectos** mix a **hectoliter** of water with a **hectogram** of sand.

They trudge down the ridge with the sand and water. After they dump it, their boat slides joyfully ahead a **hectometer!** A **hectometer** is *roughly* the length of a regulation football field. That's a pretty long distance! Nevertheless, the riverbed's width is longer – a lot longer than a **hectometer**. The brothers underestimated how much water and sand they needed. How discouraging!

The pressure is now on the fattest brother (**Kilo Liter**), the heaviest brother (**Kilo Gram**), and longest brother (**Kilo Meter**). The other brothers, sisters, and cousins have failed in their attempts. Remember the **Milli** sisters could only get the boat to move *about* the width of the eyelash? These **Kilo** boys *have* to get this raft to go a *million* times farther than a **millimeter** because *they* are a **million times bigger**! They need to move their raft a **kilometer**! A **kilometer** is *just about* 5/8 of a mile.

As **Kilo Meter** holds his eyebrows together and thinks as hard as he can, he loses focus. His foot is in pain. There is a rock lodged between his toes. Ouch! Picking the rock away gives him an idea! He and his brothers must dislodge **tons** of rocks from the ridge to start an avalanche and get that pond water to spill over. The sand will come, too! The boys estimate there should be at least a **kilogram** of sand. That would be *roughly* 2.2 pounds in mass/weight. It appeared to them that there was *about* a **kiloliter** of water. A very large hot tub completely filled with water *might be* a close approximation.

Kilo Meter works with his two brothers, **Kilo Gram** and **Kilo Liter**. One brother pries out a rock. The other two brothers wiggle surrounding rocks until they become loose. One rock tumbles down narrowly escaping the family. Another rock topples next to the first, then another and then another. The rockslide is now in motion and is becoming dangerous.

They scream out to all their smaller brothers and sisters to board the raft as quickly as they can. A quick survey of the small avalanche tells them this plan IS going to work! First they call the girls: the **Millis**. Then, the sisters who are ten times bigger than the **Millis** – the **Centis** – come running! Then, the girls who are ten times bigger than the **Centis** and 100 times bigger than the **Millis** -- the **Decis** skedaddle toward their brothers. The **Kilo** brothers scream for the remaining brothers -- all the **Deka** and **Hecto** brothers start sprinting to the raft, too!

Thousands of rocks dislodge! The kids feel the shaking earth. Dradnats, the ogre, feels it, too! Dradnats runs so fast that thorns push up into his feet. He can't let those little brats get away! He gets close enough that his deep roar rumbles in the air. His soup is boiling back at his cave, and he's just now ready to put those obnoxious kids in the kettle for flavoring!

The **Kilo** brothers watch the water and sand pour over the craggy cliff. A **kiloliter** of water (*approximately* the size of a large hot tub) and a **kilogram** of sand (that would be *about* 2.2 pounds) propel the raft forward with such force that it travels a full **kilometer!** A **kilometer,** once again, is *just about* 5/8 of a mile-- *just* the right amount of distance to get them home! They only have a second to look back and see the evil Dradnats shaking his fist and disappearing under water. "Boy, he's uglier than I ever imagined!" yells **Hecto Liter.**

"**Milli, Centi, Deci, Deka, Hecto, Kilo!** Yes, you're all here!" Each set of happy parents starts counting their kids (There have to be **six** children in each family.). "All **eighteen** kids are here!" cry **Mr.** and **Mrs. Meter, Mr.** and **Mrs. Liter, and Mr.** and **Mrs. Gram**. The kids' best **SI** friends are *also* there to anchor the raft and help them to safety. Their names are: **Ampere, Kelvin, Newton, Pascal, Joule, and Watt**.

As the parents lament their lack of judgment, **Kilo Gram** puts into words what all the kids feel. "We've gone many a time with no problem! We love you! It's not your fault! At least we now know where the ogre lives and we can steer clear of him!"

A long time passes before another trip. The raft turns moldy with holes. The SI Metric Kids save every coin they possibly can and march into the Resale Sailboat Shop the next year. They find a great looking vessel that fits them all comfortably. Soon, it will be time for another adventure!

Interesting Facts and Activities

1. Look at the ogre's name backwards. Dradnats is Standard. Standard/Customary units are used in the U.S. However, 95% of the rest of the world uses SI. The reason many countries use SI (International System of Units) instead of Standard is because this measurement system is based on powers of ten and uses decimals and zeroes so that conversions are easier. In SI, they use the meter, Liter, and gram. Just *think* of all the names we use! Here are just a few: ounce, pound, cup, pint, quart, inch, foot, yard, mile, etc. What are some others? **Also,** we have to memorize the numbers that go with these units, and each one is very different.

2. World leaders get together and use English as their common written language and SI as their common math and international commerce language. Countries want U.S. products in SI. Interchangeable parts would be easier if the whole world used SI.

3. Google the date for National Metric Week. There are many places you can search to get activities for SI. The United States Metric

Association has many activities available to young people. Check out us-metric.org or google "Metric Activities" and find a wealth of information.

4. If you look in your kitchen, laundry room, or bathroom, you will **definitely** find more than 20 products that show the measurement using the meter, Liter, and gram! Pick up something and look carefully for the Standard (U.S.) measurement, and you will *also* see the metric. Are you able to read the metric measurement? Isn't it about time you become familiar with **SI's** meter, Liter, and gram?

Guided Practice

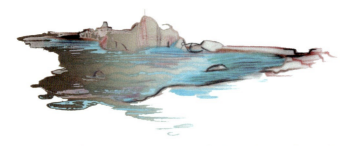

Go to the back cover of the book. Study the abbreviations in three columns. You need to really know these before you start to do the following problems or activities. Just remember the story. Milli is mm, centimeter is cm, etc. You should be able to look away from the book and say all these in order before you proceed: milli, centi, deci, (meter, Liter, gram), deka, hecto, kilo. There should be no hesitation as you recall them. Also, always keep in mind each one (say, milli and centi) is **10X bigger or 10X smaller.** You're never adding! As you touch milli, you say "1", centi "10", deci "100", (meter, Liter, gram) "1,000", etc. By the time you touch kilo, you will be at one million. As mentioned in the story, a kilo is 1,000,000 times bigger than a milli.

Study the conversion chart on page 28. Study this conversion chart for at least three minutes. Notice the bottom step starts with **milli**, the middle step is the **meter, Liter,** or **gram**, and the top step is **kilo**. In the story, the **meter**, **Liter**, and **gram** were the parents. Pay close attention that as you move up the steps, you divide! As you move down the steps, you multiply! The chart has an orange arrow. Point with a pencil where you find "multiply or divide by ten." Then, put your pencil point on the arrow. Just as in our Standard conversions, smaller units to bigger mean **divide.** For example: g = _____ kg You're going to divide! kg = _____ g You're going to multiply!

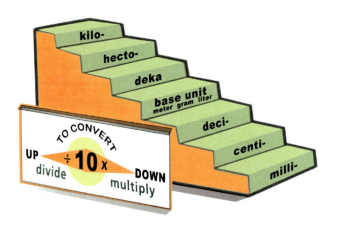

As you convert, say, 50 mg to _____ cg, you DIVIDE since you're going from smaller to bigger. Touch with your pencil and index finger to mg and cg on the chart. That's one step on the chart. Therefore, in that problem, 50 mg = 5 cg 50 mg is 10 times **smaller** (Put your pencil on the mg and your finger on the cg of the chart). When you divide using powers of ten, you simply "knock off" one zero! If there were no zeroes to "knock off", you would be moving a decimal point to the left.

Now, think 5 cg = _____mg This time you will MULTIPLY since you are going from a bigger unit to a smaller unit. Touch your pencil and index finger to the same two steps. One step difference – therefore, multiply by 10. What is 5 X 10? 5 cg = 50 mg

Try these two problems that are very similar using your index finger and pencil to mark the steps on the chart. 40 hL = _____ L (multiply) You're going down **two** steps so add **two** more zeroes. Notice you **don't count** the **hecto** step. That's how we get two steps down. What is 40 hL=_____L? (Multiplying in powers of ten, you simply add two zeros for the two steps down.)

600 mL = _____ dL (divide) You're NOT going to count the "milli" step. You're going up **two** steps; therefore you "knock off" two zeroes. This "knocking off" for division is a simple way

to divide when using powers of ten 600mL = _____dL

Try the following problems **still using the chart on page 28.** Answers for these problems will follow shortly, but try to do them on your own. Take out a piece of paper, double space, and put a), b), c) -- all the way through g). **Keep the step chart open so it can help you figure out the conversions!!** The answers will be following, but *you* try to figure them out yourself. *Then, make up more problems until you get really good at it!* Teach your parents and give them problems you make! They get to use the chart, too!

a. 7 kg = _____mg You are standing on the **kilo** step. You are going to have to step down 6 steps, right? **You do not count the kilo step!!** Look at the orange arrow chart in front of the steps. Multiplying or dividing?   As you touch each step, **think of each step as a zero**.   That would be six zeroes.   What's the answer?   Yep!

7kg = _____mg!

b. 8 kL = _____L You are on that same **kilo** step. You have to go down 3 steps.   You're going from bigger to smaller so you multiply. **Remember, don't count the kilo step.** That's 3 zeroes you will be adding to the number 8.   This is the shortcut way of multiplying by powers of ten. It's also important to think the kL is 10X bigger than hL which is 10X, bigger than daL which is 10X bigger than the L.   **10 X 10 X 10 = 1,000** Go back to your 8. Yup! 8 kL = _____L!

c. Now, 14 dam= _____ m?   You start at "dam". **da** in **dam** means means **deka! dam would be dekameter.** Start on that step.   You step **down one**...that means you're going to do what?   Remember, as you count the steps, you are NOT adding. Big to small? Multiply! (And, that's what we have here!)   Small to big? Divide!

d. 22 dg = _____g? (**Remember just a "d" means "deci" "da" is "deka"**) Put your pencil on **deci** and your index finger on the step that says **base unit**: meter, liter, gram. One step up means? Look at the orange arrow in front of the steps. Answer? 22 dg = _____ g

e. 523 mL= _____ cL? Position your pencil point and finger. One step up! Check your chart. Remember 523 is really 523 with a decimal **after** it. Move the decimal one to the left to divide. 523 mL = _____ cL? You can figure it out!

f. 315 cg = _____ kg You're going to be **dividing**. Why? You're going from smaller (cg) to bigger (kg). You're on the "**centi** step." <u>**Not counting** that step</u>, how many steps up? 5! And, isn't 315 *really* 315 with the decimal point **after** it? Yes! So to divide, you start at the decimal and count over 1, 2, 3 numbers to the **left**.

   Moving a decimal to the right is multiplying. Moving a decimal to the left is <u>dividing</u>! Oh, no! Remember you need to move 5 to the left (divide)? You've used three spaces. You have to *add* two zeroes to have your five spaces filled. Therefore, 315 cg = .00315kg Now, *that's* getting to be a hard conversion problem! However, I'm sure you were able to do it.

g. 472 hL = _____ cL Put your pencil and your finger on **hecto** and **centi** on the steps of the chart. Going bigger to smaller, you _____. Stepping down 4, means adding 4 zeroes. Be sure to put your commas in correctly. Should be easy! Go to your 472, and add 4 zeroes. 472 hL = _____cL

h. 6 m = _____dm? Multiply? Divide? (Remember "d" is "deci" ; "da" is deka) How many steps down? Would the answer be 60, . 6, 6, or .006?

Here are **ANSWERS** to problems where the answer is not given: 4,000 L ; 6 dL ; 7,000,000 mg ; 8,000 L ; 140 m ; 2.2 g ; 52.3 cL ; 4,720,000 cL; 60 dm

Phew! Enough conversions! Now! What is wrong with these? 24 L = _____mm? 72 kg = _____ hm? The first one is Liters and meters. The second one is grams and meters. No, No! If you're working with Liters, stick to the Liter family. So, that should read 24L = _____mL If you're working with grams, stick to the Gram Family ! The second one would correctly read 72 kg = _____hg In the first one, you can't mix L with m Those are two different families. In the second one, it's mixing grams with meters. Therefore, when you make additional problems at home, stick to the correct family!

More Activities

1. Remember this mnemonic device: **m**ary **c**arter **d**ecided **M**onday **d**aniel **h**ad **k**isses:

m, c, d, M, da, h, k :   **m**m, **c**m, **d**m, **M, dam, hm, km** This will help you remember all the prefixes for the meter with the **Meter** right in the middle! You can also use this for the L/ liter and the g/ gram. Try to fill in these blanks? mL, _____, dL, L, daL _____, kL Now more blanks for the gram: mg, _____, _____, _____, dag, _____, _____.

2. Some suggestions of everyday objects were given in the story. Take a sheet of paper and fold it into thirds. In the left hand column at the top put Meter, in the center at the top put Liter, and on the top of the third column on the right put Gram. Under Meter, **double space** and put: mm, cm, dm, M, dam, hm, km Under Liter put: mL, cL, dL, L, daL, hL, kL. Do this same pattern for the third column, Gram. **Go back in the story** and write down names of objects that are *very roughly* the same size – such as mm = *about the* width of an eyelash, mL = *about the* size of a drop of water, cm = *about the* width of a small finger…Get the idea? You should find quite a few comparisons used in the story.

Get with a partner and try to fill in the blanks that are left with everyday objects *always thinking ten times smaller or ten times bigger.* **You don't have to be exact! You're just trying to think of something *roughly* the same size as each metric unit.** It's important to remember that these things you take down from the book or think of yourself–- they may not be exact, but they are easy to remember, and you're not trying to be scientific at this point.

3. Make a game. Draw squares that weave around from a START to a FINISH. After the word START, in each square, put this pattern: mL, cL, dL, L, daL, hL, kL You could actually do the meter or gram if you wish. Repeat pattern as many times as you can until you reach your square for FINISH. One die. Roll to see who goes first. As you land on a square, you must say the full name such as "milliliter." You can stutter, think a bit, or correct yourself, but if you pass by the square without **fully** saying the whole word and your partner can correct you with the answer, you go back five spaces or to

START – whichever is closer. If your partner can't say it correctly, he/she goes back, too!   If neither student knows the abbreviation on the square, ask the teacher or student referee (who *really knows* the right answers) to come over and tell you. After being told the correct answer, students still go back to start. Proceed until one student lands exactly on FINISH. If FINISH is three squares away and student rolls "four", student must remain where he/she is.

5. Stand next to your desk. Start clapping in a rhythm with three beats before you talk. When teacher starts, say with the teacher: millimeter (then 4 claps), centimeter (4 claps), decimeter (4 claps), METER (4 claps), dekameter (4 claps), etc. up to kilometer. Repeat this rhythm using Liter and gram. Can you figure out how you might be able to march in place to it? March in place three times. Milligram! (march 3 times) Centigram!, etc. Repeat your march to the Liter and to the gram.

6. Stand next to your desk. Show millimeter by taking your two index fingers and having

practically no space between them. Everyone says "millimeter" **quietly.** Show centimeter by putting about a finger's width between your two index fingers and saying "centimeter" all together -- a little louder. Show decimeter by putting fingers about a crayon's distance and saying "decimeter" a little louder than centimeter. Say "meter" by stretching out your arms (about a yard's length) and saying in a classroom voice, "meter." Now, put your arms at a 45 ° angle and say "dekameter." Act like you're showing muscles when saying "dekameter" louder than a classroom voice. Raise those arms a little higher and say "hectometer!" in a loud voice. Raise those arms with your fists as high as you can and as loudly as you can, say "Kilometer!"

7. SNAP THE CARD GAME WITH METRIC You'll need twelve or more large black magic markers. Ask parents to bring in old decks of cards. It doesn't matter if the decks are complete. You'll need roughly 30 decks of cards. Teacher puts students in pairs. Give each pair of students 56 cards. Using the black marker, write the following on the side of the card with the number or

face. Write **mm** on 8 cards. Then, make 8 **cm** cards, 8 **dm**, 8 **M**, 8 **dam**, 8 **hm**, and 8 **km** The two students shuffle the 56 cards really well. Deal half the cards to the opponent. Decide who goes first. Cards are shuffled and turned over so students can't see metric prefixes written. First person puts a card down, then next person puts one down right on top of opponent's. Keep it going. When one person **puts down a larger amount** (say a dm over a cm or an M over an mm), a student slaps a hand down over the cards. Whoever slaps **first**, gets to keep the cards in the pile. If it appears to be a tie, the student's hand that is covering the card the most gets to keep all of them. Winner is person with most cards after all cards are played. Students may want to make Liter or gram cards instead.

8. There are many other activities if you just search the web. A particularly good source is the United States Metric Association at www.us-metric.org You may even be able to get freebies at times.

9. Every kid gets **_the same_** dictionary and 10 strips of paper. Each student looks through

his/her dictionary and finds pictures. If it is a picture of something your classmates know, bookmark it with a piece of paper. Teacher will take turns calling on students. If elected, student tells the class what page is needed to find one of his/her pictures. They all turn to it. Decide as a class whether that "object" would best be measured in meters, liters, or grams. Be specific. Let's say student has everyone turning to a leopard. This animal would best be measured with kg How about a garter snake? One could measure its length in cm or dm. There's no right or wrong answer. Just do reasonable estimates.

If you learn one thing from this book, know that meter measures distance, Liter measures volume, and gram measures mass/weight! Also, what if you had to make a conversion and you couldn't use the chart in the book? No problem!

On your scratch piece of paper, choose the meter, Liter, or gram. I'm going to use the gram. In a **<u>vertical</u>** column jot down: kg, hg, dag, g, dg, cg, mg Refresh your memory that if two are right next to each other, one is either ten times larger or ten times smaller. After making your column, what is the difference between an hg and a dg?* Point to each one with your index finger and your other index finger. Multiply by tens to find difference between them: 10, 100, 1000, etc.

In conversions, you'll be either adding zeroes, removing zeroes, or moving the decimal point to the right (multiply) or to the left (divide).

*You may have written grams when jotting down your list, but the same rules for conversions would apply to the Liter and the meter.

Now you know more about the meter, Liter, and gram!

Made in the USA
Coppell, TX
29 May 2021

56515706R00029